Summer Coo
101 Light and Healthy
for Busy People o

by **Vesela Tabakova**
Text copyright(c)2013 Vesela Tabakova

Table Of Contents

3

Family Friendly Summer Recipes to Suit All Tastes and Budgets

Hot summer days. Lazy summer evenings. Children playing and laughing in the warm summer twilight. Families preparing dinner and gathering around the table.

What are your favorite summertime recipes? What are the meals that your mother and grandmother made and you still love and serve?

This is my summer cookbook. The recipes I share with you are my family's all time favorites and are always part of our summer rituals. I hope you enjoy them and maybe a few will become part of your best summer evenings!

Summer Salad Recipes

Shopska Salad

Serves 5-6

Ingredients:

3-4 tomatoes, diced

1 large cucumber, peeled and diced

1-2 fresh green peppers, cut

1 small onion, finely cut

1 cup grated cheese

for the dressing:

2 tbsp red wine vinegar

3 tbsp sunflower or olive oil

salt, to taste

10 black olives, to serve

Directions:

In a salad bowl, gently combine the peppers with the diced tomatoes, cucumbers and onion. Add in salt, oil, vinegar and stir.

Serve topped with grated feta cheese and garnished with black olives.

Chicken and Lettuce Salad

Serves 6-7

Ingredients:

2 cups cooked chicken, coarsely chopped

1/2 head iceberg lettuce, sliced and chopped

1 celery rib, chopped

1 medium apple, chopped

1/2 red bell pepper, deseeded and chopped

6-7 green olives, pitted and halved

1 red onion, chopped

for the dressing:

1/2 cup mayonnaise

1 tbsp honey

2 tbsp lemon juice

salt and pepper, to taste

Directions:

Cut all the vegetables and toss them together with the olives in a large bowl. Chop the already cooked and cooled chicken into small pieces and add it to the salad.

Prepare the salad dressing in a separate smaller bowl by mixing together the mayonnaise, honey and lemon juice.

Season with salt and pepper to taste and serve.

Chicken Salad with Quinoa

Serves 5-6

Ingredients:

1 cup quinoa

2 cups water

2 cups chicken breast, cooked and chopped

1/2 cup black olives, pitted

1 tbsp capers, chopped

1 garlic clove, minced

2 tbsp olive oil

2 tbsp lemon juice

1/2 cup parsley, finely cut

salt, to taste

ground black pepper, to taste

Directions:

Wash very well quinoa in lots of water and cook it according to package directions. Set aside to cool.

Combine olives and all other ingredients in a large bowl, stirring well. Add in quinoa, toss to combine and serve.

Grilled Chicken and Avocado Salad

Serves 4

Ingredients:

2 cups grilled skinless, boneless chicken breast, diced

2 avocados, peeled, pitted and diced

1 red onion, finely chopped

1/2 cup green olives, pitted

10 cherry tomatoes

2 tbsp lemon juice

3 tbsp olive oil

1 tsp oregano

salt and black pepper, to taste

Directions:

In a medium bowl, combine the avocados, chicken, onion, and cherry tomatoes. Season with oregano, salt and pepper to taste.

Add the olives, lemon juice and olive oil and toss lightly to coat.

Chicken, Broccoli and Cashew Salad

Serves 6

Ingredients:

1 lb fresh broccoli, cut in florets

1 cup grilled boneless chicken breast, diced

1/2 cup cashews, baked

2 tbsp sunflower seeds, salted and baked

2 tbsp Parmesan cheese, grated

1/2 cup fresh parsley leaves, finely cut

2 tbsp olive oil

2 tbsp lemon juice

Directions:

Wash broccoli florets and steam them for five minutes until just tender then transfer into a large salad bowl. Set aside to cool.

Add chicken, cashews, sunflower seeds and the finely cut parsley.

In a smaller cup, mix the olive oil and lemon juice.

Pour over the salad and serve sprinkled with Parmesan cheese.

Mediterranean Chicken Pasta Salad

Serves 6-8

Ingredients:

3 cups medium pasta, cooked

1 small roasted chicken, skin and bones removed, shredded

1 cup cherry tomatoes

1 cucumber, halved, sliced

1 red bell pepper, sliced

1 small red onion, sliced

1/3 cup fresh basil leaves, finely chopped

1/3 cup parsley, finely cut

1 cup black olives, pitted

1/3 cup pine nuts, toasted

for the dressing

3 tbsp red wine vinegar

4-5 tbsp cup olive oil

1 garlic clove, crushed

salt, to taste

Directions:

Place pasta, chicken, tomato, cucumber, bell pepper, onion, basil, parsley, olives and pine nuts in a large bowl.

Make the dressing by combining vinegar, oil, garlic and salt. Pour the dressing over the salad and toss to combine.

Light Italian Beef and Spinach Salad

Serves 6

Ingredients:

8 oz deli Italian roast beef, cut into 1/ 4 inch strips

1 red onion, sliced and separated into rings

2 tomatoes, sliced

1 red pepper, sliced

6 cups baby spinach leaves or fresh spinach, torn

2 tbsp olive oil

1/2 cup grated Parmesan cheese, to serve

for the dressing:

1/2 cup sour cream

1 tbsp mustard

2 garlic cloves, crushed

Directions:

Stir together all dressing ingredients in a deep bowl and set aside.

Warm olive oil in a large skillet and sauté beef and onions. Cook for 2-3 minutes, stirring occasionally, over medium heat until beef is heated through.

Toss together beef, spinach, tomatoes, red pepper and dressing in a large salad bowl. Serve sprinkled with Parmesan cheese.

Mediterranean Beef Salad

Serves 4

Ingredients:

8 oz roast beef, thinly sliced

6 cups mixed greens, torn

1 cucumber, cut

6-7 fresh white button mushrooms, thinly sliced

4 tbsp fresh basil leaves, torn

2 tbsp balsamic vinegar

4 tbsp olive oil

1 tsp salt

Directions:

Prepare the dressing by mixing vinegar, olive oil, crushed garlic, salt and basil leaves in a bowl.

Divide greens among four plates. Arrange beef with cucumbers and mushrooms on top. Drizzle with dressing and serve.

Turkey Pasta Salad

Serves 6

Ingredients:

1 cup small pasta, uncooked

1 cup skinless lean turkey breast, cooked, diced

1 small red onion, chopped

2 carrots, diced and cooked

1 cup green peas, cooked

2 tbsp olive oil

1 tbsp white wine vinegar

salt and black pepper, to taste

Directions:

Cook pasta according to package directions. Drain well after rinsing with cold water. Set aside.

Place turkey, onion, carrots, and peas in a salad bowl and toss to combine. Add in cooked pasta.

Whisk olive oil, vinegar, salt and pepper in a separate bowl. Pour over the pasta salad and stir. Cover and chill until ready to serve.

Pasta Salad wit Tuna and Green Beans

Serves 4

Ingredients:

1 cup medium pasta

9 oz green beans, trimmed and cut into 2 inch lengths

1 cup cherry tomatoes, halved

1 ripe avocado, cubed

1 can tuna, drained and broken into big chunks

1/4 cup olive oil

2 tbsp lemon juice

2 tsp Dijon mustard

a pinch of sugar

Directions:

Cook pasta in boiling water for 10 minutes. Add the green beans and cook for 4 more minutes. Drain and cool.

Prepare the dressing by combining together olive oil, lemon juice, mustard and a pinch of sugar. Season with salt and black pepper to taste.

Combine pasta, beans, cherry tomatoes, avocado, tuna and the dressing. Toss gently and serve.

Tuna and Lettuce Salad

Serves 4

Ingredients:

1 head green lettuce, washed and drained

1 cucumber, peeled and sliced

1 can tuna, drained and broken into big chunks

1/2 cup canned sweet corn, drained

a bunch of radishes, sliced

a bunch of spring onions, finely cut

juice of half lemon or 2 tbsp of white wine vinegar

3 tbsp sunflower or olive oil

salt, to taste

Directions:

Cut the lettuce into thin strips. Slice the cucumber and the radishes as thinly as possible and chop the spring onions.

Mix all the vegetables in a large bowl, add the tuna and the sweet corn and season with lemon juice, oil and salt to taste.

Salmon Macaroni Salad Recipe

Serves 6-7

Ingredients:

2 cups macaroni pasta

1 cup canned salmon pieces

1 red pepper, cut into strips

1/2 cup canned sweet corn, drained

1/2 cup mayonnaise

1 tsp mustard

1 tsp lemon juice

1 bunch spring onions, chopped

3 tbsp fresh parsley leaves, finely cut

1 tbsp fresh dill, finely cut

freshly ground black pepper, to taste

Directions:

Cook macaroni according to package directions. Remove from heat, drain, rinse briefly in cold water and drain again.

In a large bowl mix the salmon, corn, red pepper, mayonnaise, mustard, and lemon juice. Mix in the spring onions, parsley and dill. Add the cooked pasta while it is still warm.

Season with freshly ground pepper to taste. Serve chilled.

Sausage, Tomato and Pasta Salad

Serves 6

Ingredients:

1 1/2 cup spiral pasta

2 tbsp sunflower oil

1 lb pork sausages

2 zucchinis, sliced lengthwise

1 1/2 cups cherry tomatoes

1 cup small mozzarella cheese, sliced

4 tbsp olive oil

4 tbsp lemon juice

1 tsp dried basil

Directions:

Cook pasta following package directions, until al dente. Drain and transfer to a bowl. Stir in two tablespoons of oil. Set aside to cool.

Grill sausages, turning, for ten minutes or until just cooked through. Set aside to cool slightly and slice thickly.

Grill zucchinis, until char-grilled. Transfer to a plate. Grill tomatoes for one minute.

Combine sausages, zucchinis, tomatoes and mozzarella with pasta.

Prepare the dressing by combining lemon juice, olive oil and basil. Drizzle over salad and stir. Season with salt and pepper and toss to combine. Serve warm.

Potato, Pancetta and Asparagus Salad

Serves 6

Ingredients:

2 lbs spring potatoes, washed, peeled, halved lengthwise

4 tbsp olive oil

2 garlic cloves, crushed

6 slices mild pancetta

1 bunch asparagus, trimmed and cut diagonally into 2 inch lengths

1/2 cup green beans, cut into 2 inch lengths

1 tbsp red wine vinegar

2 tbsp sunflower oil

1 tbsp mustard

1/4 cup spring onions, finely cut

salt and black pepper, to taste

Directions:

Preheat oven to 350 F. Combine potatoes, two tablespoons of olive oil and garlic in a large baking dish. Season with salt and pepper to taste and bake turning occasionally, for about twenty minutes or until golden brown.

Heat a large frying pan over medium heat. Cook the pancetta slices for one minute each side or until crisp. Drain and transfer to a plate. Cook the asparagus and green beans in salted boiling water for three minutes or until bright green and tender crisp. Drain.

Break the pancetta into large pieces. Place in a large serving bowl along with the potatoes, asparagus, green beans and spring onions.

Combine the remaining oil, vinegar and mustard in a small bowl. Season with salt and pepper and pour over the salad. Gently toss and serve.

Shepherds' Salad

Serves 6

Ingredients:

5-6 tomatoes, diced

2 cucumbers, sliced

5-6 white button mushrooms, sliced

2 red bell peppers, sliced

7 oz ham, diced

1 onion, chopped

4 eggs, boiled and sliced

7 oz feta cheese, grated

1/2 cup parsley, finely cut

4 tbsp olive oil

1 tbsp vinegar

1 tsp salt

20-30 black olives

Directions:

Combine tomatoes, cucumbers, peppers, mushrooms, ham and onions in a salad bowl. Drizzle with olive oil and vinegar, add salt and toss to combine.

Split the salad in six plates and sprinkle with the grated feta cheese and finely chopped parsley.

Boil the eggs for ten minutes, then cut them in discs. Garnish the six salad plates with egg slices and olives. Serve chilled.

Summer Avocado Salad

Serves 4-5

Ingredients:

1 large avocado, peeled and sliced

3-4 small red tomatoes, quartered

2-3 small yellow tomatoes, quartered

a handful of rocket leaves

3 tbsp olive oil

1 tbsp lemon juice

salt and black pepper, to taste

Directions:

Place avocado, rocket and tomatoes in a salad bowl.

Season with salt and black pepper, drizzle with lemon juice and olive oil, and stir to combine.

Quinoa and Black Bean Salad

Serves 6

Ingredients:

1 cup quinoa

1 cup black beans, cooked, rinsed and drained

1/2 cup sweet corn, cooked

1 red bell pepper, deseeded and chopped

4 spring onions, chopped

1 garlic clove, crushed

1 tbsp dry mint

2 tbsp lemon juice

1/2 tsp salt

1 tbsp apple vinegar

4 tbsp olive oil

Directions:

Rinse quinoa in a fine sieve under cold running water until water runs clear. Put quinoa in a pot with two cups of water.

Bring to a boil, then reduce heat, cover and simmer for fifteen minutes or until water is absorbed and quinoa is tender. Fluff quinoa with a fork and set aside to cool.

Put beans, corn, bell pepper, spring onions and garlic in a bowl and toss with vinegar and black pepper to taste. Add in quinoa and toss well again.

In a separate bowl whisk together lemon juice, salt and olive oil and drizzle over salad. Toss well and serve.

Roasted Vegetable Quinoa Salad

Serves 6

Ingredients:

2 zucchinis, cut into bite sized pieces

1 eggplant cut into bite sized pieces

3 roasted red peppers, cut into bite sized pieces

4-5 small white button mushrooms, whole

1 cup quinoa

1/2 cup olive oil

1 tbsp apple cider vinegar

1/2 tsp dried oregano

salt and pepper to taste

7 oz feta, crumbled

Directions:

Toss the zucchinis, mushrooms and eggplant in half the olive oil, salt and pepper. Place onto a baking sheet in a single layer and bake in a preheated 350 F oven for 30 minutes flipping once.

Wash well, strain and cook the quinoa following package directions.

Prepare the dressing from the remaining olive oil, apple cider vinegar, oregano, salt and pepper.

In a big bowl combine quinoa, roasted zucchinis, eggplant, mushrooms, roasted red peppers, and feta.

Toss the dressing into the salad and serve.

Quinoa with Oven Roasted Tomatoes and Pesto

Serves 6

Ingredients :

for the salad

1 cup dry quinoa

2 cups water

1 cup cherry tomatoes, for roasting

1/2 cup cherry tomatoes, fresh

1 avocado, cut into chunks

1/2 cup black olives, pitted

1 cup mozzarella cheese, cut into bite size pieces

for the pesto

1 clove garlic, chopped

1/2 tsp salt

1/2 cup walnuts, toasted

1 cup basil leaves

1 tbsp lemon juice

1 tbsp mustard

4-6 tbsp olive oil

1 tsp summer savory

2 tbsp water (optional)

Directions:

Preheat the oven to 350 F. Line a baking sheet with foil. Make sure the tomatoes are completely dry, then drizzle with olive oil and savory and toss to coat them all. Bake the tomatoes for about 20 minutes, flipping once, until they are brown. Sprinkle with salt.

Rinse quinoa very well in a fine mesh strainer under running water; set aside to drain. Place two cups of water and quinoa in a large saucepan over medium-high heat. Bring to the boil then reduce heat to low. Simmer for 15 minutes. Set aside, covered, for ten minutes and fluff with a fork.

Make the pesto by placing garlic, walnuts and 1/2 teaspoon salt in a food processor. Add basil, mustard and lemon juice and blend in batches until smooth. Add oil, one tablespoon at a time, processing in between, until the pesto is lightened and creamy. For an even lighter texture you can add two tablespoons of water. Taste for salt and add more if you like.

In a large mixing bowl, gently mix the quinoa with the tomatoes, avocado, olives and mozzarella pieces. Spoon in the pesto and toss to distribute it evenly.

Fresh Vegetable Quinoa Salad

Serves 6

Ingredients:

1 cup quinoa

2 cups water

a bunch of fresh onions, chopped

2 green peppers, chopped

1/2 cup black olives, pitted and chopped

2 tomatoes, diced

1 cup raw sunflower seeds

3 tbsp olive oil

4 tbsp fresh lemon juice

1 tbsp dried mint

Directions:

Prepare the dressing by combining olive oil, lemon juice, and dried mint in a small bowl and mixing it well. Place the dressing in the refrigerator until ready to use.

Wash well and cook quinoa according to package directions. When it is ready leave it aside for ten minutes, then transfer it to a large bowl. Add the diced peppers, finely cut fresh onions, olives and diced tomatoes stirring until mixed well.

Stir the dressing (it will have separated by this point) and add it to the salad, tossing to evenly coat. Add salt and pepper to taste and sprinkle with sunflower seeds.

Warm Mushroom Quinoa Salad

Serves 4-5

Ingredients:

1 cup quinoa

2 cups vegetable broth

1 tbsp sunflower oil

2-3 spring onions, chopped

2 garlic cloves, chopped

10 white button mushrooms, sliced

1-2 springs of fresh rosemary

1/2 cup dried tomatoes, chopped

2 tbsp olive oil

salt and freshly ground pepper

1/2 cup fresh parsley, finely cut

Directions:

Wash well the quinoa in plenty of cold water, strain it and put it in a saucepan. Add vegetable broth and bring to the boil. Lower heat and simmer for 10 minutes until the broth is absorbed.

Heat oil in a frying pan and sauté onions for 2-3 minutes. Add garlic and sauté for another minute. Add sliced mushrooms and season with salt and pepper. Finally, add the rosemary. Stir fry the mushrooms until soft.

Mix well the cooked quinoa with the mushrooms and tomatoes. Serve sprinkled with fresh parsley.

Spicy Buckwheat Vegetable Salad

Serves 4-5

Ingredients:

1 cup buckwheat groats

2 cups vegetable broth

2 tomatoes, diced

1/2 cup spring onions, chopped

1/2 cup parsley leaves, finely chopped

1/2 cup fresh mint leaves, very finely chopped

1/2 yellow bell pepper, chopped

1 cucumber, peeled and cut into 1/4-inch cubes

1/2 cup cooked or canned brown lentils, drained

1/4 cup freshly squeezed lemon juice

1 tsp hot pepper sauce

salt, to taste

Directions:

Heat a large, dry saucepan and toast the buckwheat for about three minutes. Boil the vegetable broth and add it carefully to the buckwheat. Cover, reduce heat and simmer until buckwheat is tender and all liquid is absorbed (5-6 minutes). Remove from heat, fluff with a fork and set aside to cool.

Chop all vegetables and add them together with the lentils to the buckwheat. Mix the lemon juice and remaining ingredients well and drizzle over the buckwheat mixture. Stir well to distribute the dressing evenly.

Buckwheat Salad with Asparagus and Roasted Peppers

Serves 4-5

Ingredients:

1 cup buckwheat groats

1 3/4 cups vegetable broth

1/2 lb asparagus, trimmed and cut into 1 in pieces

4 roasted red bell peppers, diced

2-3 spring onions, finely chopped

2 garlic cloves, crushed

1 tbsp red wine vinegar

3 tbsp olive oil

salt and black pepper, to taste

1/2 cup fresh parsley leaves, finely cut

Directions:

Heat a large, dry saucepan and toast the buckwheat for about three minutes. Boil the vegetable broth and add it carefully to the buckwheat. Cover, reduce heat and simmer until buckwheat is tender and all liquid is absorbed (five-seven minutes). Remove from heat, fluff with a fork and set aside to cool.

Rinse out the saucepan and then bring about an inch of water to a boil. Cook the asparagus in a steamer basket or colander, for 2-3 minutes or until tender.

Transfer the asparagus in a large bowl along with the roasted peppers. Add in the spring onions, garlic, red wine vinegar, salt, pepper and olive oil. Stir to combine. Add the buckwheat to the vegetable mixture.

Sprinkle with parsley and toss the salad gently. Serve at room temperature.

Roasted Broccoli Buckwheat Salad

Serves 4-5

Ingredients:

1 cup buckwheat groats

1 3/4 cups water

1 head of broccoli, cut into small pieces

1 lb asparagus, trimmed and cut into 1 in pieces

1/2 cup roasted cashews

1/2 cup basil leaves, minced

1/2 cup olive oil

2 garlic cloves, crushed

3 tbsp Parmesan cheese, grated, to serve

Directions:

Arrange vegetables on a baking sheet and drizzle with olive oil. Roast in a preheated to 350 F oven for about 15 minutes or until tender.

Heat a large, dry saucepan and toast the buckwheat for about three minutes, or until it releases a nutty aroma. Boil the water and add it carefully to the buckwheat. Cover, reduce heat and simmer until buckwheat is tender and all liquid is absorbed (5-6 minutes). Remove from heat, fluff with a fork and set aside to cool.

Prepare the dressing by blending basil leaves, olive oil, garlic, and salt.

Toss vegetables, buckwheat and dressing together in a salad bowl. Add in cashews and serve sprinkled with Parmesan cheese.

Haloumi, Lentil and Rocket Salad

Serves 4

Ingredients:

1 cup brown lentils, cooked and drained

1 cup cherry tomatoes, halved

2 cucumbers, halved and thinly sliced

1/2 cup baby rocket leaves

1/2 red onion, finely cut

1 tbsp lemon juice

1 tsp honey

4 tbsp olive oil

6 oz haloumi, cut into slices

Directions:

Combine the lentils, tomatoes, cucumber, rocket leaves and onion in a salad bowl. Whisk together lemon juice, honey, olive oil, salt and pepper in a small bowl. Drizzle the dressing over the salad and toss to coat.

Pat the haloumi dry with a paper towel and toss in the remaining olive oil. Heat a frying pan over medium heat and cook the haloumi in batches, for 1-2 minutes each side or until golden. Transfer to a plate.

Divide the salad among serving plates. Top with haloumi and serve.

Blue Cheese Iceberg Salad

Serves 6

Ingredients:

1 small iceberg salad

1 avocado, cut

1 cucumber, cut

1 red onion, cut

1/2 cup walnuts, raw

5.5 oz blue cheese, coarsely crumbled

¼ cup orange juice

3 tbsp olive oil

1 tbsp honey

salt, to taste

Directions:

Tear the iceberg lettuce or cut it in thin strips. Toss it in a medium salad bowl together with the other vegetables.

Add the coarsely crumbled blue cheese and walnuts.

Whisk together honey, orange juice, olive oil and salt, drizzle over the salad and serve.

Apple, Walnut and Radicchio Salad

Serves 4

Ingredients:

2 radicchio, trimmed, finely shredded

2 apples, quartered and thinly sliced

4 spring onions, chopped

1/2 cup walnuts, roasted

1 tbsp mustard

1 tbsp lemon juice

1/3 cup olive oil

Directions:

Prepare the dressing by combining mustard, lemon juice and olive oil.

Place walnuts on an oven tray and roast in a preheated to 400 F oven for three-four minutes or until brown.

Mix radicchio, apples, onions and walnuts in a large salad bowl. Add the dressing and toss to combine.

Snow White Salad

Serves 4

Ingredients:

1 large or two small cucumbers -fresh or pickled

4 cups of plain yogurt

1/2 cup of crushed walnuts

2-3 cloves garlic, crushed

1/2 bunch of dill

3 tbsp sunflower oil

salt, to taste

Directions:

Strain the yogurt in a piece of cheesecloth or a clean white dishtowel. You can suspend it over a bowl or the sink.

Peel and dice the cucumbers, place in a large bowl. Add the crushed walnuts and the crushed garlic, the oil and the finely chopped dill. Scoop the drained yogurt into the bowl and stir well.

Add salt to the taste, cover with cling film, and put in the fridge for at least an hour so the flavors can mix well.

Fresh Greens Salad

Serves 8

Ingredients:

1 head red leaf lettuce, rinsed, dried and chopped

1 head green leaf lettuce, rinsed, dried, and chopped

1 head endive, rinsed, dried and chopped

1 cup frisee lettuce leaves, rinsed, dried, and chopped

3 leaves fresh basil, chopped

3 sprigs fresh mint, chopped

4 tbsp. olive oil

2 tbsp lemon juice

1 tbsp honey

salt, to taste

Directions:

Place the red and green leaf lettuce, frisee lettuce, endive, basil, and mint into a large salad bowl and toss lightly to combine.

Prepare the dressing from lemon juice, olive oil and honey and pour over the salad. Season with salt to taste.

Fried Zucchinis with Yogurt Sauce

Serves 4

Ingredients:

4 medium zucchinis, peeled and sliced

2 cups yogurt

3 cloves garlic, crushed

a bunch of fresh dill, chopped

1 cup sunflower oil

1 cup flour

salt, to taste

Directions:

Start by combining the garlic and chopped dill with the yogurt in a bowl. Add salt to taste and put in the fridge.

Wash and peel the zucchinis, and cut them in thin diagonal slices or in rings 1/4 in thick. Salt and leave them in a suitable bowl placing it inclined to drain away the juices.

Coat the zucchinis with flour, then fry turning on both sides until they are golden-brown (about 3 minutes on each side). Transfer to paper towels and pat dry.

Serve the zucchinis hot or cold, with the yogurt mixture on the side.

Roasted Eggplant and Peppers Salad

Serves 4

Ingredients:

2 medium eggplants

2 red or green bell peppers

2 tomatoes

3 cloves garlic, crushed

fresh parsley

1-2 tbsp red wine vinegar

olive oil, as needed

salt, pepper

Directions:

Wash and dry the vegetables. Prick the skin off the eggplants. Bake the eggplants, tomatoes and peppers in a pre-heated oven at 480 F for about forty minutes until the skins are well burnt.

Take out of the oven and leave in a covered container for about ten minutes. Peel the skins off and drain well the extra juices. Deseed the peppers.

Cut all the vegetables into small pieces. Add the garlic and mix well with a fork or in a food processor. Add olive oil, vinegar and salt to taste. Stir again. Serve cold and sprinkled with parsley.

Cheese Stuffed Tomatoes

Serves 4

Ingredients:

4 large tomatoes

9 oz feta cheese

1 tsp paprika

Directions:

Cut the top of each tomato in such a way as to be able to stuff the tomato and cover with the cap. Scoop out the seeds and central part of the tomatoes to create a hollow.

Mash the scooped out parts of the tomatoes, add to the feta cheese and stir to make a homogeneous mixture. Add paprika.

Stuff the tomatoes with the mixture and cover with the caps. Serve chilled, garnished with sprays of parsley.

Mozzarella, Tomato and Basil Couscous Salad

Serves 4

Ingredients:

4 tomatoes, diced

1 cup fresh mozzarella cheese, diced

3-4 spring onions, very finely cut

2 tbsp olive oil

1 tbsp lemon juice

salt, to taste

1/4 teaspoon fresh ground black pepper

1 garlic clove, crushed

1 cup couscous

1 1/4 cups water

1/2 cup chopped fresh basil

Directions:

In a big salad bowl combine tomatoes, mozzarella, salt, pepper, garlic, lemon juice, olive oil and spring onions. Toss everything well, cover, and marinate for half an hour.

Boil the water and pour over the couscous. Set aside for five minutes then fluff with a fork. Add couscous to the tomato mixture along with the chopped basil leaves and toss again.

Summer Soup Recipes

Creamy Carrot Soup

Serves 6-7

Ingredients:

10 carrots, peeled and chopped

1 medium onion chopped

4-5 cups water

2 cloves garlic, minced

5 tbsp olive oil

½ cup heavy cream

salt and pepper, to taste

2 cups croûtons, to serve

Directions:

Heat the olive oil in a large soup pot over medium heat and gently sauté the onions, carrots and garlic. Add in 4-5 cups of water and bring to a boil.

Reduce heat to low and simmer for 30 minutes. Transfer the soup to a blender or food processor and blend until smooth. Return to the pot and continue cooking for a few more minutes. Remove soup from heat, stir in the cream, and serve with croûtons sprinkled over each serving.

Spanish Gazpacho Soup

Serves 6

Ingredients:

2.25 lb tomatoes, peeled and halved

1 onion, sliced

1 green pepper, sliced

1 big cucumber, peeled and sliced

2 cloves garlic

salt, to taste

4 tbsp olive oil

1 tbsp red wine vinegar

to garnish,

½ onion, chopped

1 green pepper, chopped

1 cucumber, chopped

Directions:

Place the tomatoes, garlic, onion, green pepper, cucumber, salt, olive oil and vinegar in a blender or food processor and puree until smooth, adding small amounts of cold water if needed to achieve desired consistency.

Serve the gazpacho chilled with the chopped onion, green pepper and cucumber sprinkled over each serving.

Avocado Gazpacho

Serves 4

Ingredients:

2 ripe avocados, peeled, pitted and diced

1 cup tomatoes, diced

1 cup cucumbers, peeled and diced

1 small onion, chopped

10 oz chicken broth

2 tbsp lemon juice

1 tsp salt

black pepper, to taste

Directions:

Place avocados, cucumbers, tomatoes, onion, broth, lemon juice and salt and pepper in a blender.

Blend until smooth and serve sprinkled with cilantro or parsley leaves.

Cold Cucumber Soup

Serves 4-5

Ingredients:

1 large or two small cucumbers

2-3 cups yogurt

2-3 cloves garlic, crushed or chopped

2 cups cold water

4 tbsp sunflower or olive oil

1 cup dill, finely chopped

1/2 cup crushed walnuts

Directions:

Wash the cucumber, peel and cut into small cubes.

In a large bowl, dilute the yogurt with water to taste, add the cucumber and garlic; stir to combine.

Add salt to the taste, garnish with dill and crushed walnuts and put in the fridge to cool.

Chicken and Quinoa Soup

Serves 4

Ingredients:

2 chicken breasts, diced

1 large onion, diced

2 cloves garlic

1-2 celery ribs, diced

1-2 carrots, diced

1 tsp paprika

1 bay leave

1/2 cup quinoa, rinsed

4 cups water

salt and pepper, to taste

lemon juice, to serve

Directions:

Heat olive oil in a large pot and gently sauté onions, carrots, celery and garlic. Pour in water, add chicken, season with salt and pepper to taste, and bring to the boil.

Reduce heat and simmer slowly until cooked through. Add quinoa and simmer for 10 minutes more. Serve with lemon juice.

Mediterranean Chicken Soup

Serves 6-8

Ingredients:

about 1.5 lb chicken breasts

3-4 carrots, chopped

1 celery rib, chopped

1 red onion, chopped

1/3 cup rice

6 cups water

10 black olives, pitted and halved

fresh parsley or coriander, to serve

1/2 tsp salt

ground black pepper, to taste

lemon juice, to serve

Directions:

Place chicken breasts in a soup pot. Add onion, carrots, celery, salt, pepper and water. Stir well and bring to a boil. Add rice and olives, stir and reduce heat. Simmer for 30-40 minutes.

Remove chicken from the pot and let it cool slightly. Shred it and return it back to the pot. Serve soup with lemon juice and sprinkled with fresh parsley or coriander.

Beef and Vegetable Minestrone

Serves 6-7

Ingredients:

2 slices bacon, chopped

1 cup lean ground beef

2 carrots, chopped

2 cloves garlic, finely chopped

1 large onion, chopped

1 celery rib, chopped

1 bay leaf

1 tsp dried basil

1 tsp dried rosemary, crushed

1/4 tsp crushed chillies

1 cup canned tomatoes, chopped

3 cups beef broth

1 cup canned chickpeas, drained

½ cup small pasta

Directions:

In a large saucepan, cook bacon and ground beef until well done, breaking up the beef as it cooks. Drain off the fat and add carrots, garlic, onion and celery.

Cook for about 5 minutes, or until the onions are translucent. Season with the bay leaf, basil, rosemary and crushed chillies. Stir in tomatoes and beef broth.

Bring to a boil then reduce heat and simmer for about 20 minutes.

Add the chickpeas and pasta. Cook uncovered, for about 10 minutes, or until the pasta is ready.

Bulgarian Meatball Soup

Serves 8

Ingredients:

1 lb lean ground beef

3-4 tbsp flour

1 onion, chopped

2 garlic cloves, cut

1 tomato, diced

2 potatoes, diced

1 green pepper, chopped

4 cups water

5.5 oz vermicelli, broken into pieces

½ bunch of parsley, finely cut

3 tbsp olive oil

½ tsp black pepper

1 tsp summer savory

1 tsp paprika

1 tsp salt

yogurt, to serve

Directions:

Combine ground meat, savory, paprika, black pepper and salt in a large bowl. Mix well with hands and roll teaspoonfuls of the mixture into balls. Put flour in a small bowl and roll each meatball in the flour, coating entire surface then set aside on a large plate.

Heat olive oil into a large soup pot and sauté onion and garlic until transparent. Add water and bring to the boil over high heat. Add meatballs, carrot, green pepper and potatoes.

Reduce heat to low and simmer, uncovered, for 15 minutes. Add tomato, parsley and vermicelli and cook for 5 more minutes.

Serve with a dollop of yogurt on top.

Easy Fish Soup

Serves 6-7

Ingredients:

1 lb white fish fillets cut in small pieces

9 oz scallops

1 onion, chopped

3 tomatoes, chopped

2 potatoes, diced

1 red pepper, chopped

2 carrots, diced

1 garlic clove, crushed

1/2 cup parsley, finely cut

3 tbsp olive oil

a pinch of cayenne pepper powder

1 tsp dried oregano

1 tsp dried thyme

1 tsp dried dill

½ tsp pepper

½ cup white wine

4 cups water

1/3 cup heavy cream

Directions:

Heat the olive oil over medium heat and sauté the onion, red pepper, garlic and carrots until tender. Stir in the cayenne, herbs, salt, and pepper.

Add the white wine, water, potatoes and tomatoes and bring to a boil.

Reduce heat, cover, and cook until the potatoes are almost done. Stir in the fish and the scallops and cook for another 10 minutes.

Stir in the heavy cream and parsley and serve hot.

Spanish Seafood Soup

Serves 4-5

Ingredients:

2.25 lb whole raw prawns

3 cups cold water

3 spring onions, chopped

1 bell pepper, finely chopped

2 large tomatoes, diced

1 tbsp tomato puree

2 garlic cloves, minced

2 tbsp olive oil

2 bay leaves

1 tsp paprika

½ tsp cayenne pepper

salt and pepper, to taste

the juice of one small lemon

1/2 cup parsley, finely cut

Directions:

De-head and de-shell the prawns and leave them in a bowl to the side. Put the heads and shells in a pan with cold water. Add the bay leaves, bring to the boil and reduce heat. Simmer for 20 minutes.

While the broth is simmering sauté the shallots and pepper in olive oil for 5 minutes, then add the garlic for two more minutes. When the broth is ready strain it and add it to the the shallots.

Bring to the boil, add the tomatoes and tomato puree, the prawns, the mussels and simmer for 10 more minutes.

In the end add paprika and cayenne pepper, season to taste with salt and pepper and add the lemon juice. Garnish with parsley and serve.

Italian Minestrone

Serves 5-6

Ingredients:

1 cup cabbage, chopped

2 carrots, chopped

1 celery rib, thinly sliced

1 small onion, chopped

2 garlic cloves, chopped

1 tbsp olive oil

4 cups water

1 cup canned tomatoes, diced, undrained

1 beef bouillon cube

1 cup fresh spinach, torn

½ cup pasta, cooked

black pepper and salt, to taste

Directions:

Sauté carrots, cabbage, celery, onion and garlic in oil for 5 minutes in a deep saucepan. Add water, tomatoes and bouillon and bring to a boil.

Reduce heat and simmer uncovered, for 20 minutes or until vegetables are tender. Stir in spinach, macaroni and season with pepper and salt to taste.

Spinach, Leek and Quinoa Soup

Serves 6

Ingredients:

½ cup quinoa

2 leeks halved lengthwise and sliced

1 onion, chopped

2 garlic cloves, chopped

2 tbsp sunflower oil

1 can tomatoes, diced, undrained

2 cups fresh spinach, cut

2 cups vegetable broth

2 cups water

1 tsp paprika

salt and pepper, to taste

Directions:

Heat a large pot over medium heat. Add oil and onion and sauté for 2 minutes, add leeks and cook for another 2-3 minutes, then add garlic and paprika and stir.

Season with salt and pepper to taste. Add the vegetable broth, water, canned tomatoes, and quinoa.

Bring to a boil then reduce and simmer for 10 minutes. Stir in spinach and cook for another 5 minutes.

Tomato Soup

Serves 4

Ingredients:

4 cups chopped fresh tomatoes or 2 cups canned tomatoes

1 large onion, diced

1/2 cup vermicelli

3 cups water

4 garlic cloves, minced

3 tbsp olive oil

1 tsp salt

½ tsp black pepper

1 tsp sugar

½ cup fresh parsley, finely cut

Directions:

Sauté onions and garlic in oil in a large soup pot. When onions have softened, add tomatoes and cook for 15-20 minutes until tomatoes are soft. Stir in the spices.

Blend the soup then return it to the pot, add in water, vermicelli and a teaspoon of sugar and bring to boil. Lower heat and simmer for 10 minutes, stirring occasionally. Sprinkle with parsley and serve.

Mushroom Soup

Serves 4

Ingredients:

2 cups white button mushrooms, peeled and chopped

1 onion, chopped

2 cloves garlic, crushed and chopped

1 tsp dried thyme

3 cups vegetable broth

salt and pepper, to taste

4 tbsp olive oil

Directions:

Sauté onions and garlic in a large soup pot till transparent. Add thyme and mushrooms.

Cook for 10 minutes, then add the vegetable broth and simmer for another 10-20 minuets. Blend, season and serve.

French Vegetable Soup

Serves 4

Ingredients:

1 leek, thinly sliced

1 large zucchini, diced

1 cup green beans, cut into short lengths

2 garlic cloves, cut

3 cups vegetable broth

1 cup canned tomatoes, chopped

3.5 oz vermicelli, broken into small pieces

3 tbsp olive oil

black pepper to taste

4 tbsp freshly grated Parmesan cheese

Directions:

Sauté the leek, zucchini, green beans and garlic for about 5 minutes. Add the vegetable broth. Stir in the tomatoes and bring to the boil, then reduce heat.

Add black pepper to taste and simmer for 10 minutes, or until the vegetables are tender but still holding their shape. Stir in the vermicelli. Cover again and simmer for a further 5 minutes.

Serve warm sprinkled with Parmesan cheese.

Potato Soup

Serves 5-6

Ingredients:

4-5 medium potatoes, peeled and chopped

2 carrots, chopped

1 zucchini, chopped

1 celery rib, chopped

3 cups water

3 tbsp olive oil

1 cup whole milk

½ tsp dried rosemary

salt to taste

black pepper, to taste

1/2 cup fresh parsley for garnish, finely cut

Directions:

Heat the olive oil over medium heat and sauté the vegetables for 2-3 minutes. Pour 3 cups of water, add the rosemary and bring the soup to a boil, then lower heat and simmer until all the vegetables are tender.

Blend soup in a blender until smooth. Add a cup of warm milk and blend some more. Serve warm, seasoned with black pepper and parsley sprinkled over each serving.

Broccoli, Zucchini and Blue Cheese Soup

Serves 5-6

Ingredients:

2 leeks, white part only, sliced

1 head broccoli, coarsely chopped

2 zucchinis, chopped

1 potato, chopped

2 cups vegetable broth

2 cups water

3 tbsp olive oil

3.5 oz blue cheese, crumbled

1/3 cup light cream

Directions:

Heat the oil in a large saucepan over medium heat. Sauté the leeks, stirring, for 5 minutes or until soft. Add bite sized pieces of broccoli, zucchinis, potato, water and broth and bring to a boil. Reduce heat to low and simmer, stirring occasionally, for 10 minutes, or until vegetables are just tender. Remove from heat and set aside for 5 minutes to cool slightly.

Transfer soup to a blender. Add the cheese and blend in batches until smooth. Return to saucepan and place over low heat. Add cream and stir to combine. Season with salt and pepper to taste.

Lentil, Barley and Mushroom Soup

Serves 4

Ingredients*:*

2 medium leeks, trimmed, halved, sliced

10 white button mushrooms, sliced

3 garlic cloves, cut

2 bay leaves

2 cans tomatoes, chopped, undrained

3/4 cup red lentils

1/3 cup barley

3 tbsp olive oil

1 tsp paprika

1 tsp savory

½ tsp cumin

Directions:

Heat oil in a large saucepan over medium-high heat. Sauté leeks and mushrooms for 3 to 4 minutes or until softened. Add cumin, paprika, savory and tomatoes, lentils, barley, and 5 cups cold water. Season with salt and pepper.

Cover and bring to the boil. Reduce heat to low. Simmer for 35-40 minutes, or until barley is tender.

Spinach Soup

Serves 4-5

Ingredients:

14 oz frozen spinach

1 large onion or 4-5 scallions

1 carrot, chopped

4 cups water

3-4 tbsp olive oil

1/4 cup white rice

1-2 cloves garlic, crushed

black pepper and salt, to taste

Directions:

Heat the oil in a cooking pot, add the onion and carrot and sauté together for a few minutes, until just softened. Add chopped garlic and rice and stir for a minute. Remove from heat.

Add the spinach along with about 2 cups of hot water and season with salt and pepper. Bring back to a boil, then reduce the heat and simmer for around 30 minutes.

Cream of Spinach Soup with Feta Cheese

Serves 4

Ingredients:

14 oz frozen spinach

5.5 oz feta cheese

1 large onion or 4-5 scallions

2 -3 tbsp light cream

3-4 tbsp olive oil

1-2 cloves garlic

3 cups water

black pepper and salt, to taste

Directions:

Chop the onion and spinach. Heat the oil in a cooking pot, add the onion and spinach and sauté together for a few minutes, until just softened. Add garlic and stir for a minute. Remove from heat.

Add about 2 cups of hot water and season with salt and pepper. Bring back to the boil, then reduce the heat and simmer for around 30 minutes.

Blend soup in a blender. Crumble the cheese with a fork. Stir in the crumbled feta cheese and the cream. Serve hot.

Nettle Soup

Serves 6

Ingredients:

1.5 lb young top shoots of nettles, well washed

3-4 tbsp sunflower oil

2 potatoes, diced small

1 bunch spring onions, coarsely chopped

1 ½ cup freshly boiled water

1 tsp salt

Directions:

Clean the young nettles, wash and cook them in slightly salted water. Drain, rinse, drain again and then chop or pass through a sieve.

Sauté the chopped spring onions and potatoes in the oil until the potatoes start to color a little.

Turn off the heat, add the nettles, then gradually stir in the water. Stir well, then simmer until the potatoes are cooked through.

Thick Herb Soup

Serves 4

Ingredients:

3.5 oz parsley

3.5 oz dill

1.75 oz mint leaves

1.75 oz celery leaves

4 tbsp butter or olive oil

2 tbsp plain flour

3 cups. water

½ cup thick yogurt or sour cream

juice of a lemon

2 egg yolks

1 tsp salt

Directions:

Wash the herbs, remove stalks and snip or chop finely. Heat butter or oil in a cooking pot, add prepared herbs, cover and simmer gently.

When the herbs are tender, add flour, stir well. Cook for a few moments before slowly adding the water, stirring all the time. Simmer for about 10-15 min.

Mix separately egg yolks, thick yogurt (or sour cream) and lemon juice. Add to the soup slowly, then stir well. The soup should not be allowed to boil any more.

Summer Main Dish Recipes

Ratatouille

Serves 4

Ingredients:

1 eggplant, cut into small cubes

2 large tomatoes, chopped

2 zucchinis, sliced

1 onion, sliced into rings

1 green pepper, sliced

6-7 sliced white button mushrooms

3 cloves garlic, crushed

2 tsp dried parsley

½ cup Parmesan cheese

3 tbsp olive oil

Directions:

Place eggplant pieces on a tray and sprinkle with plenty of salt. Let sit for 30 minutes, then rinse with cold water.

Heat olive oil in an ovenproof casserole over medium heat. Gently sauté garlic for a minute or two. Add in parsley and eggplant. Continue sautéing until eggplant is soft. Sprinkle with a tablespoon of Parmesan cheese.

Spread zucchinis in an even layer over the eggplant. Sprinkle with a little more cheese.

Continue layering onion, mushrooms, pepper and tomatoes, covering each layer with a sprinkling of Parmesan cheese. Bake in a preheated to 350 F oven for 40 minutes.

Greek Style Chicken Skewers

Serves 4

Ingredients:

1.5 lb chicken breast fillets, cut in bite size pieces

2 tbsp olive oil

1 large lemon, juiced

2 garlic cloves, crushed

1 tsp dried oregano

1 tsp dried rosemary

Directions:

Thread chicken pieces onto skewers. Place in a shallow dish. Combine olive oil and lemon juice, garlic and oregano. Pour over chicken. Turn to coat. Marinate for 40 minutes if time permits.

Preheat a barbecue plate on medium-high heat. Cook skewers for 3 minutes each side or until chicken is just cooked through. Serve with vegetable salad and feta cheese.

Hunter Style Chicken

Serves 4-6

Ingredients:

1 chicken (3-4 lbs), cut into pieces

2 tbsp olive oil

2 medium onions, thinly sliced

1 red bell pepper, cut

6-7 white button mushrooms, sliced

2 cups canned tomatoes, diced and drained

3 garlic cloves, thinly sliced

salt and freshly ground pepper

1/3 cup white wine

1/2 cup parsley leaves, finely cut

1 tsp sugar

Directions:

Rinse chicken pieces and pat dry. Heat olive oil in a large skillet on medium heat. Working in batches cook the chicken pieces until nicely browned, 5-6 minutes, then turn over and brown the other side. Transfer chicken to a bowl and set aside.

Drain off all of the rendered fat. Add 2 tbsp of olive oil and sauté the sliced onions and bell pepper for a few minutes. Add the mushrooms and cook some more until onion is translucent. Add garlic and cook a minute more.

Add wine and simmer until liquid is reduced by half. Add tomatoes and a tsp of sugar and stir.

Place the chicken pieces on top of the tomatoes and onions, skin side up. Lower the heat and cover the skillet with the lid slightly ajar. Simmer the chicken for about 40 minutes, turning from time to time, until the meat is almost falling off the bones. Sprinkle with parsley, set aside for 3-4 minutes and serve.

Moroccan Chicken with Almond and Spinach Couscous

Serves 4

Ingredients:

4 chicken breast fillets, halved

4 tbsp olive oil

1 tsp saffron

1 tsp nutmeg

1 tsp cinnamon

1 red bell pepper, deseeded, chopped

1 cup baby spinach leaves

1/4 cup slivered almonds

1/4 cup raisins

1 cup chicken broth

1 cup couscous

Directions:

Toss chicken breasts in olive oil and sprinkle with cinnamon, nutmeg and saffron. Heat a frying pan over medium heat. Add the chicken and cook for 4 minutes each side or until golden. Transfer to a baking dish and bake in a preheated to 350 F oven for 10 minutes or until cooked through.

Heat the oil and gently sauté the bell pepper and silvered almonds, stirring, for 2 minutes. Add the raisins and chicken broth and bring to the boil. Remove from heat and add the couscous. Use a fork to combine.

Cover and set aside for 2-3 minutes. Use a fork to fluff the grains.

Fold through spinach until just wilted. Serve the couscous topped with sliced chicken.

Easy Chicken Paella

Serves 4

Ingredients:

4 chicken thigh fillets, trimmed and cut into pieces

1 red onion, chopped

1 large red bell pepper, chopped

11/2 cups rice

2 cups chicken broth

1/2 cup frozen peas, thawed

1/2 cup parsley leaves, finely cut

1 tbsp paprika

1/2 tsp saffron

2 tbsp boiling water

2 tbsp olive oil

lemon wedges, to serve

Directions:

Place saffron in a small cup and add two tablespoons of boiling water. Set aside for 5 minutes.

Heat olive oil in a large saucepan over high heat and cook chicken 3-4 minutes or until golden. Add in onion and cook some more. Add paprika, red pepper and rice and stir to combine. Add saffron mixture, green peas and chicken broth then bring to a boil.

Reduce heat to low and simmer, covered, stirring from time to time, for 10-15 minutes, or until rice is just tender. Serve with lemon wedges.

Chicken and Artichoke Rice

Serves 4

Ingredients:

3 skinless chicken breasts, cut into strips

2 leeks, white parts only, chopped

7-8 canned artichokes hearts, quartered

2 garlic cloves, crushed

2/3 cup rice

2 cups chicken broth

2 tbsp olive oil

1 tsp lemon rind

7-8 fresh basil leaves, chopped

1 bay leaf

juice of 1 lemon

Directions:

Heat the oil in a large saucepan over low heat. Gently sauté the leeks, bay leaf and garlic for about 3-4 minutes, stirring occasionally. Add in the lemon rind and the chicken breasts and cook, stirring, for 5-6 minutes. Add rice, stir, add chicken broth and half the lemon juice.

Bring a the boil then reduce heat, cover, and cook for 10 minutes. Set aside covered for 5 minutes then stir in the chopped basil, artichokes hearts and remaining lemon juice.

Easy Chicken Parmigiana

Serves 4

Ingredients:

4 chicken breast fillets

1 eggplant, peeled and sliced lengthwise

1 can tomatoes, diced

9 oz mozzarella cheese, sliced

2 tbsp olive oil

Directions:

In an ovenproof casserole, heat olive oil and brown the chicken pieces. Place eggplant over the chicken and add in tomatoes.

Top with mozzarella slices and bake in a preheated to 350 F for 20 minutes or until cheese is golden.

One-Pot Chicken Dijonnaise

Serves 4

Ingredients:

4 chicken breasts with skin

1 onion, sliced

5-6 white button mushrooms, sliced

2 garlic cloves, crushed

1 tbsp flour

1/3 cup Dijon mustard

1/3 cup mayonnaise

1/3 cup dry white wine

1/3 cup chicken broth

1/2 cup sour cream

2 tbsp olive oil

2 tbsp finely chopped tarragon

salt and pepper, to taste

Directions:

Heat oil in an ovenproof casserole over medium heat. Cook chicken in batches for 2-3 minutes each side until golden. Add onion and sauté for 3 more minutes or until soft. Stir in the mushrooms and garlic and cook, stirring, for a further minute. Add in flour and stir to combine. Add wine, mayonnaise, Dijon mustard, chicken broth and tarragon and combine well.

Cover with a lid or foil and bake in a preheated to 380 F oven for 10-15 minutes or until chicken is cooked through and the liquid has evaporated. Add in sour cream, salt and black pepper to taste and heat through.

Sweet and Sour Sicilian Chicken

Serves 4

Ingredients:

4 chicken thigh fillets

1 large red onion, sliced

3 garlic cloves, chopped

2 tbsp flour

1/3 cup dry white wine

1 cup chicken broth

1/2 cup green olives

2 tbsp olive oil

2 bay leaves

1 tbsp fresh oregano leaves

2 tbsp brown sugar or honey

2 tbsp red wine vinegar

salt and black pepper, to taste

Directions:

Combine the flour with salt and black pepper and coat well all chicken pieces. Heat oil in ovenproof casserole and cook the chicken in batches, for 1-2 minutes each side, or until golden.

Add in onion, garlic, and wine and cook, stirring for 1 more minute. Add the chicken broth, olives, bay leaves, oregano, sugar and vinegar and bake, in a preheated to 380 F oven, for 20 minutes, or until the chicken is cooked through.

Lemon Rosemary Chicken

Serves 4

Ingredients:

4 boneless skinless chicken breasts or 4-6 tights

2 garlic cloves, crushed

4-5 lemon slices

1 tbsp capers

1 tbsp dried rosemary

3 tbsp olive oil

salt and pepper, to taste

Directions:

Heat olive oil in a skillet over medium-low heat and sauté the garlic for about a minute. Add the lemon slices to the bottom of the skillet and lay the chicken breasts on top of the lemon.

Add rosemary, capers, season with salt and pepper to taste, cover, and cook, on medium-low, for 20 minutes or until the chicken breasts are cooked through. Uncover and cook for 2-3 minutes, until the liquid evaporates.

Chicken and Zucchini Frittata

Serves 4

Ingredients:

1 cup chicken, chopped finely

3 green onions, finely chopped

1 garlic clove, chopped

1 zucchini, peeled and diced

1 tomato, diced

2 tbsp dill, finely chopped

5 eggs

1 cup grated Parmesan cheese

3 tbsp olive oil

Directions:

In and ovenproof pan, heat olive oil and gently cook the chicken until almost cooked through. Add in the onion and garlic and cook for another minute, stirring.

Add the zucchini and tomato and cook for for 3-4 minutes, until lightly cooked.

In a medium bowl, whisk eggs, Parmesan cheese and dill together. Pour over the top of the chicken and vegetable mixture, making sure that it covers it well. Bake in a preheated to 360 F oven for around 15 minutes, until set. Garnish with fresh dill.

Spanish Marinated Skewers

Serves 4

Ingredients:

2 lbs beef, cut into 1 inch cubes

1 onion, chopped

4 garlic cloves, chopped

2 tbsp parsley, chopped

1 tbsp paprika

1/2 cup olive oil

1/3 cup dry red wine

2 cups small white button mushrooms, whole

for the dressing:

1 tbsp paprika

2 tbsp red wine vinegar

1/2 cup olive oil

1 tbsp fresh rosemary leaves

Directions:

Place the beef cubes in a bowl together with the chopped onion and garlic. Add wine, paprika, parsley and olive oil. Mix thoroughly and marinate for at least an hour.

Thread beef onto skewers, dividing the cubes with mushrooms. Grill on a hot barbecue, turning, until cooked through.

Prepare the dressing by combining paprika, vinegar, oil and rosemary. Place skewers on plates and drizzle dressing on top. Serve with fresh salad and/or rice.

Beef and Spinach Stew

Serves 4

Ingredients:

1 lb stewing beef

10 oz frozen spinach

1 onion, chopped

3 garlic cloves, crushed

1 cup beef broth

1/2 cup canned tomatoes, drained

4 tbsp olive oil

6 oz butter

1 tbsp paprika

salt and pepper, to taste

Directions:

In a large stew pot, heat the butter and olive oil and seal the beef pieces. Add onion and garlic and sauté for a few minutes.

Add in paprika, beef broth and bring to the boil then reduce heat and simmer, covered, for 30-40 minutes. Stir in tomatoes and spinach and cook, uncovered, for 10 minutes. Serve over rice or couscous.

Beef Kebabs

Serves 4

Ingredients:

2 lbs ground beef

2 onions, grated

1 tsp cumin

1 tsp dried oregano

1 tbsp dried parsley

Directions:

Preheat a barbecue or char-grill on medium-high. Combine the ground beef, onions and herbs in a bowl. Roll tablespoonfuls of the mixture into balls. Thread 4-5 meatballs onto 1 skewer. Repeat to make 12 kebabs.

Cook the kebabs for about 2-3 minutes each side for medium cooked. Transfer to a plate, cover with foil and set aside for 5 minutes to rest.

Salmon Kebabs

Serves 4

Ingredients:

2 shallots, ends trimmed, halved

6 skinless salmon fillets, cut into 1 inch pieces

3 limes, cut into thin wedges

Directions:

Preheat barbecue or char grill on medium-high. Thread shallot, salmon and lime wedges onto each skewer.

Repeat to make 12 kebabs. Bake the kebabs for about 3 minutes each side for medium cooked. Transfer to a plate, cover with foil and set aside for 5 minutes to rest.

Swordfish Kebabs

Serves 4

Ingredients:

2 zucchinis, cut in 2x2 inch cubes

2 lbs skinless swordfish steaks, cut into 2 inch cubes

1 cup cherry tomatoes

1/2 cup basil leaves, finely chopped

4 garlic cloves, crushed

juice from one lemon

rind from 1 lemon

olive oil cooking spray

salt and black pepper, to taste

Directions:

Prepare marinade by combining garlic, lemon rind, lemon juice, basil leaves and salt and pepper in a small bowl. Thread fish cubes onto skewers, then zucchinis and tomatoes.

Place skewers in a shallow plate. Brush with marinade and refrigerate for 30 minutes if time permits.

Spray skewers with olive oil spray and bake on a preheated barbecue plate on medium heat. Bake for 6-7 minutes, turning, or until fish is just cooked through.

Pork Kebabs

Serves 6

Ingredients:

6 (2 lbs) pork loin medallions, cut into 2 inch cubes

2 red peppers, deseeded, cut into 2 inch pieces

30 white button mushrooms, whole

Directions:

Preheat your barbecue or char grill on medium-high. Thread pork, pepper and mushrooms onto 1 skewer. Repeat to make 12 kebabs.

Cook the kebabs for about 2-3 minutes each side for medium cooked. Transfer to a plate, cover with foil and set aside for 5 minutes to rest.

Grilled Vegetable Skewers

Serves: 4

Ingredients:

1 red pepper

1 green pepper

3 zucchinis, halved lengthwise and sliced

3 onions, quartered

12 medium mushrooms, whole

2 garlic cloves, crushed

2 tbsp olive oil

1 tsp summer savory

1 tsp cumin

1 spring fresh rosemary, leaves only

salt and ground black pepper, to taste

Directions:

Deseed and cut the peppers into chunks. Divide between 6 skewers threading alternately with the zucchinis, onions and mushrooms. Set aside the skewers in a shallow plate.

Mix the crushed garlic with the herbs, cumin, salt, black pepper and olive oil. Roll each skewer in the mixture. Bake them on a hot barbecue or char grill, turning occasionally, until slightly charred.

Potato and Zucchini Bake

Serves: 6

Ingredients:

1½ lb potatoes, peeled and sliced into rounds

5 zucchinis, peeled and sliced into rounds

2 onions, sliced

3 tomatoes, pureed

½ cup water

4 tbsp olive oil

1 tsp dried oregano

1/3 cup fresh parsley leaves, chopped

salt and black pepper, to taste

Directions:

Place potatoes, zucchinis and onions in a large, shallow ovenproof baking dish. Pour over the the olive oil and pureed tomatoes. Add salt and freshly ground pepper to taste and toss the everything together. Add in water.

Bake in a preheated to 350 F oven for an hour, stirring halfway through.

Okra and Tomato Casserole

Serves: 4-5

Ingredients:

1 lb okra, stem ends trimmed

4 large tomatoes, cut into wedges

3 garlic cloves, chopped

3 tbsp olive oil

1 tsp salt

black pepper, to taste

Directions:

In a large casserole, mix together trimmed okra, sliced tomatoes, olive oil and chopped garlic. Add salt and pepper and toss to combine.

Bake in a preheated to 350 F oven for 45 minutes, or until the okra is tender.

Zucchini and Rice Stew

Serves 4

Ingredients:

2 lbs zucchinis, diced

1 cup green onions, finely chopped

5 tbsp sunflower oil

2 cups water

2 tomatoes, diced

1 tsp salt

1 tsp paprika

salt and black pepper, to taste

2½ cups water

1 cup chopped fresh dill

Directions:

Gently sauté green onions in oil and a little water. Transfer onions in a baking dish, add zucchinis, tomatoes, rice, salt, paprika, pepper and water.

Stir, cover with a lid or foil and bake in preheated to 350 F oven for 30 minutes, or until rice is done. Sprinkle with dill.

Spinach with Rice

Serves 4

Ingredients:

1.5 lb fresh spinach, washed, drained and chopped

1/2 cup rice

1 onion, chopped

1 carrot, chopped

5 tbsp olive oil

2 cups water

Directions:

Heat oil in a large skillet and cook the onions and the carrot until soft. Add paprika and rice and stir. Add two cups of warm water stirring constantly as the rice absorbs it, and simmer for 10 minutes.

Wash the spinach cut it in strips then add to the rice and cook until it wilts. Remove from heat and season to taste.

Eggplant Casserole

Serves 4

Ingredients:

2 medium eggplants, peeled and diced

1 cup canned tomatoes, drained and diced

1 zucchini, peeled and diced

9-10 black olives, pitted

1 onion, chopped

4 garlic cloves, chopped

2 tbsp tomato paste

1 cup canned tomatoes, drained and diced

3 tbsp olive oil

1 tbsp paprika

salt and black pepper, to taste

1 cup parsley, chopped, to serve

Directions:

Heat olive oil in a deep casserole dish and gently sauté onions, garlic, and eggplants. Add in paprika and tomato paste and sauté, stirring, for 1-2 minutes. Add in the rest of the ingredients.

Cover, and bake at 350 F for 30-40 minutes. Sprinkle with parsley and serve.

Eggplant and Chickpea Casserole

Serves 4

Ingredients:

2-3 eggplants, peeled and diced

1 onion, chopped

2-3 garlic cloves, crushed

1 can chickpeas, (15 oz), drained

1 can tomatoes, (15 oz), undrained, diced

1 tsp paprika

½ tsp cinnamon

1 tsp cumin

4 tbsp olive oil

salt and pepper, to taste

1 cup grated Parmesan cheese

Directions:

Peel and dice the eggplants. Heat olive oil in a deep ovenproof casserole and sauté onions and crushed garlic. Add paprika, cumin and cinnamon. Stir well to coat evenly. Sauté for 3-4 minutes until the onions have softened.

Add the eggplant, tomatoes and chickpeas. Bake in a preheated to 350 F oven, covered, for 15 minutes, or until the eggplant is tender.

Uncover and sprinkle with Parmesan cheese. Bake for a few more minutes until the liquid evaporates and the cheese is golden.

Artichoke and Onion Frittata

Serves 4

Ingredients:

1 small onion, chopped

1 cup marinated artichoke hearts, drained

6 eggs

1 garlic clove, crushed

1 tbsp olive oil

salt and freshly ground black pepper, to taste

1/2 cup fresh parsley, finely cut, to serve

Directions:

Heat oil in a non-stick oven pan over medium heat and sauté onion stirring occasionally, for 5-6 minutes or until golden brown. Add artichokes and cook for 2 minutes or until heated through.

Whisk eggs with garlic until combined well. Season with salt and pepper. Pour the egg mixture over the artichoke mixture. Reduce heat, cover and cook for 10 minutes or until frittata is set around the edge but still runny in the center.

Place pan into preheated oven and cook 4-5 until golden brown. Remove from oven and cut into wedges. Serve sprinkled with parsley.

Mediterranean Omelette with Fennel, Olives, and Dill

Serves 6

Ingredients:

2 cups fresh fennel bulb, sliced and chopped

1 cup cherry tomatoes, halved

1/4 cup green olives, pitted

5 eggs, gently beaten with salt, black pepper and paprika

2 tbsp olive oil

1/2 tsp ground black pepper

1 tsp paprika

1/2 tsp salt

2 tbsp chopped fresh dill

Directions:

Heat one tablespoon of olive oil in a nonstick skillet over medium-high heat. Sauté fennel bulb, stirring, for 3-4 minutes or until light brown. Cover, and simmer until soft, about 5 minutes.

Add tomatoes and olives. Season with salt, pepper and paprika and sauté for 2-3 minutes more. Transfer fennel mixture to a bowl.

Heat remaining oil in the same skillet and cook beaten eggs until eggs are just set in center, tilting the skillet and lifting edges with a spatula in a way to let uncooked portion flow underneath. Cover with fennel mixture and sprinkle with dill. With the help of a spatula, fold uncovered half of omelet over; slide onto a plate and serve.

Poached Eggs with Feta and Yogurt

Serves 4

Ingredients:

12 eggs

2 cups plain yogurt

10 oz feta cheese, crumbled

2 tsp paprika

3 cloves garlic

2 oz butter

Directions:

Crush the garlic and stir together with the yogurt and the crumbled cheese. Divide the mixture into four plates.

Poach the eggs, take them out with a serving spoon and place three eggs on top of the mixture in each plate.

Brown the butter together with the paprika and pour one quarter over each plate before serving.

Mish-Mash

Serves 5-6

Ingredients:

2 small onions, chopped

1 green bell pepper, chopped

2 red bell peppers, chopped

4 tomatoes, cubed

2 garlic cloves, crushed

8 eggs

9 oz feta cheese, crumbled

4 tbsp olive oil

half a bunch parsley

black pepper, to taste

salt, to taste

Directions:

In a large pan sauté onions over medium heat, till transparent. Reduce heat and add bell peppers and garlic. Continue cooking until soft.

Add the tomatoes and continue simmering until the mixture is almost dry. Add the cheese and all eggs and cook until well mixed and not too liquid. Season with black pepper and remove from heat. Sprinkle with parsley.

Feta Cheese Stuffed Zucchinis

Serves 5-6

Ingredients:

5-6 zucchinis

3.5 oz feta cheese, crumbled

3 eggs

1 onion, finely chopped

1/2 cup milk

3.5 oz butter

salt, to taste

Directions:

Halve the peeled zucchinis lengthwise then hollow and salt them. Sauté the finely chopped onion in half of the butter.

Combine half of the milk, grated feta cheese and 1 egg in a bowl.

Stuff the zucchinis with the mixture, arrange in a baking dish and pour over the remaining 2 eggs beaten with the rest of the milk.

Bake for approximately 30 min in a preheated oven. A few minutes before the dish is ready fleck the remaining butter over the zucchinis.

Eggs and Feta Cheese Stuffed Peppers

Serves 4

Ingredients:

8 red bell peppers

6 eggs

4 oz feta cheese

a bunch of parsley

2 cups breadcrumbs

sunflower oil for frying

Directions:

Grill the peppers or roast them in the oven at 480 F. Peel and deseed the peppers.

Mix the crumbled feta cheese with 4 beaten eggs. Stuff the peppers with the mixture.

Beat the remaining two eggs. Roll each stuffed pepper first in breadcrumbs then dip in the beaten eggs. Fry in hot oil turning once. Serve sprinkled with parsley.

Feta Cheese Baked in Foil

Serves 4

Ingredients:

14 oz hard feta cheese

3 oz butter

1 tbsp paprika

1 tsp summer savory

Directions:

Cut the feta cheese into four medium-thick slices and place them on sheets of butter-lined foil.

Place cubes of butter on top each feta cheese piece, sprinkle with paprika and savory and wrap.

Place in a tray and bake in a moderate oven. Serve wrapped in the foil.

Breaded Cheese

Serves 4

Ingredients:

14 oz feta cheese

2 eggs, beaten

2 tbsp flour

3-4 tbsp breadcrumbs

vegetable oil for frying

Directions:

Cut the cheese in four equal slices. Dip each piece first in cold water, then roll in the flour, then in the beaten eggs, and finally in the breadcrumbs.

Fry the cheese pieces in preheated oil on both sides. Serve warm.

Rich Vegetable One-Pot Pasta

Serves 4

Ingredients:

12 oz dry pasta

11/2 cup tomato sauce

2 cups water

1/2 onion, finely chopped

1 cup white button mushrooms, chopped

1/3 cup black olives, pitted

1/2 small eggplant, peeled and cubed

1 red pepper, cut

3 tbsp olive oil

1 tsp dried basil

1 tsp black pepper

1 tsp salt

1/2 cup parsley, finely cut

Directions:

In a large saucepan, heat olive oil over medium-high heat. Gently sauté the finely chopped onion and red pepper for 1-2 minutes. Add in the mushrooms and eggplant and sauté for a few minutes more, stirring.

Add the tomato sauce, water, salt, pepper, basil and black olives and bring to a boil. Add in pasta, cover, and simmer for about 10 minutes or until the pasta is cooked to al dente.

Taste to adjust seasonings, sprinkle with parsley and serve.

One-Pot Broccoli Pasta

Serves 4

Ingredients:

8 oz dry pasta

1.5 lb broccoli, cut into florets

4 cups water

1/2 onion, finely chopped

4-5 white button mushrooms, chopped

2 garlic cloves, chopped

1/2 cup frozen peas

1/2 cup sweet corn

1/4 cup heavy cream

3 tbsp olive oil

1 tsp dried basil

salt and black pepper, to taste

a handful of baby rocket leaves, to serve

Directions:

Add water, pasta, broccoli, mushrooms, garlic, onion, peas and sweet corn to a large pot, set over high heat, and bring to a boil. Lower heat and simmer for 10 minutes, stirring constantly.

Add in the cream, salt and pepper to taste and simmer for 1-2 minutes more. Remove from heat and set aside for a few minutes.

Taste to adjust seasonings, sprinkle with baby rocket leaves, and serve.

Sweet Potato Spaghetti

Serves: 4

Ingredients:

12 oz spaghetti

1 sweet potato peeled, slice into quarters

1/2 small onion, sliced

2 garlic cloves, chopped

1 carrot, quartered

1 large parsnip, quartered

1 tbsp tomato paste

1 tbsp rosemary, chopped

1/2 tsp thyme

4 tbsp olive oil

1 tbsp balsamic vinegar

salt and black pepper, to taste

1 cup finely gut green onions, to serve

Directions:

Arrange sweet potatoes, onion, carrot and parsnip on a lined baking sheet. Toss it in olive oil, salt, pepper and balsamic vinegar. Roast at 380 F until the vegetables are tender, about 20 minutes.

In a large pot of boiling salted water, cook spaghetti according to package instructions. Drain and set aside in a large bowl.

Once the vegetables have cooled, purée them together with tomato paste, thyme and rosemary. Add some water as needed to get the blade moving.

Combine spaghetti with the sauce. Add spaghetti water as needed to loosen. Sprinkle with chopped green onions and serve.

Quick Orzo and Zucchini Dinner

Serves: 4-5

Ingredients:

1 cup orzo

2-3 medium zucchinis, peeled and cubed

1/2 onion

1/2 cup white wine

3 tbsp olive oil

1 tbsp dried oregano

1/3 cup fresh dill, finely cut

1 tsp salt

1 tsp fresh black pepper

2 tbsp lemon juice

Directions:

Cook orzo according to package directions (in salted water) and rinse thoroughly with cold water when you strain it. Add in a tbsp of olive oil, stir, and set aside.

Gently sauté onion and zucchinis in 2 tbsp of olive oil, stirring, until onions are translucent. Add oregano and white wine and cook uncovered on low heat for 10 minutes. Add in orzo and stir to combine well. Add lemon juice, dill, and simmer, covered for 5 more minutes.

Summer Dessert Recipes

Delicious French Eclairs

Serves 12

Ingredients:

1/2 cup butter

1 cup boiling water

1 cup sifted flour

4 eggs

a pinch of salt

Directions:

In a medium saucepan, combine butter, salt, and boiling water. Bring to the boil, then reduce heat and add a cup of flour all at once, stirring vigorously until mixture forms a ball. Remove from heat and add eggs, one at a time, whisking well to incorporate completely after each addition. Continue beating until the mixture is thick and shiny and breaks from the spoon.

Pipe or spoon onto a lined baking sheet then bake for 20 minutes in a preheated to 450 F oven. Reduce heat to 350 F and bake for 20 minutes more, or until golden. Set aside to cool and fill with sweetened whipped cream or custard.

Coconut-flavored Rice Pudding with Figs

Serves 4

Ingredients:

1 1/2 cups short-grain white rice, rinsed

1/2 cup brown sugar

8 figs, halved

3 cups boiling water

1 1/2 cups shredded coconut

1 tsp salt

1 tbsp vanilla powder

Directions:

In a heavy saucepan, bring 1 ½ cup water to a boil, then add the rice, stirring, until it boils again. Reduce the heat and simmer for 7-8 minutes, until the water is absorbed and the rice is half-cooked.

In another bowl, pour 1/12 cups boiling water over the shredded coconut, sugar, and vanilla and let it soak for 20 minutes. Drain well and pour into the rice. Bring to a boil, reduce the heat and simmer until the rice is done. Stir in the figs and serve.

Pasta with Honey and Pistachios

Serves 2

Ingredients:

1 cup cooked small pasta, warm

1 tbsp pistachio nuts, finely ground

1 tbsp butter

2 tbsp honey

3 tbsp sugar

1/2 tsp orange zest

1/2 tsp rose water

Directions:

Combine well all the ingredients in a bowl and serve warm or room temperature.

Caramel Cream

Serves 8

Ingredients:

11/2 cup sugar

4 cups cold milk

8 eggs

2 tsp vanilla powder

Directions:

Melt 1/4 of the sugar in a non-stick pan over low heat. When the sugar has turned into caramel, pour it into 8 cup-sized ovenproof pots covering only the bottoms.

Whisk the eggs with the rest of the sugar and the vanilla, and slowly add the milk. Stir the mixture well and divide between the pots.

Place the 8 pots in a larger, deep baking dish. Pour 3-4 cups of water into the dish. Place the baking dish in a preheated to 280 F oven for about an hour and bake but do not let the water boil, as the boiling will overcook the cream and make holes in it: if necessary, add cold water to the baking dish.

Remove the baking dish from the oven; remove the pots from the dish. Place a shallow serving plate on top, then invert each pot so that the cream unmolds. The caramel will form a topping and sauce.

Dark Chocolate Mousse

Serves 4

Ingredients:

4 oz dark chocolate, broken into small pieces

2 tbsp butter

a pinch of salt

2 egg yolks

4 tbsp water

1 tbsp sugar

2/3 cup heavy cream, chilled

Directions:

Put chocolate together with butter, 2 tablespoons of water and a pinch of salt in a heatproof bowl. Set this bowl over a bigger saucepan full with simmering water. When the butter and chocolate start to melt, stir gently until smooth. Set aside to cool.

Beat egg yolks, sugar and 2 tablespoons of water in another heatproof bowl over the same saucepan of simmering water. Whisk it for about 3-4 minutes, until egg yolk mixture is hot to the touch. Pour the hot egg mixture into the warm chocolate mixture and gently stir until smooth. Set over a bowl of ice to chill, whisking constantly until mixture is slightly cooler then room temperature.

Beat the 2/3 cup heavy cream until it forms soft peaks. Place half of it into the chocolate mixture and gently fold it. Add in the remaining half and continue folding until nearly all the streaks have disappeared. Divide mousse into 4 glass serving bowls, refrigerate at least 2 hours and serve.

Yogurt-Strawberries Ice Pops

Serves 8-9

Ingredients:

3 cups yogurt

3 tbsp honey

2 cups strawberries, quartered

Directions:

Strain the yogurt in a piece of cheesecloth or a clean white dishtowel. You can suspend it over a bowl or the sink.

Combine the strained yogurt with honey. Blend the strawberries with a blender then gently fold the strawberry puree into the yogurt mixture until just barely combined, with streaks remaining.

Divide evenly among the molds, insert the sticks and freeze for 3-4 hours until solid.

Blueberry Yogurt Dessert

Serves 6

Ingredients:

1/3 cup blueberry jam

1 cup fresh blueberries

2 tbsp powdered sugar

1 cup heavy cream

2 cups yogurt

1 tsp vanilla extract

Directions:

Strain the yogurt in a piece of cheesecloth or a clean white dishtowel. You can suspend it over a bowl or the sink.

In a large bowl, beat the cream and powdered sugar until soft peaks form. Add strained yogurt and vanilla and beat until medium peaks form and the mixture is creamy and thick.

Gently fold half the fresh blueberries and the blueberry jam into cream mixture until just barely combined, with streaks remaining. Divide dessert among 6 glass bowls, top with fresh blueberries and serve.

Fresh Strawberries in Mascarpone and Rose Water

Serves 4

Ingredients:

6 oz strawberries, washed

1 cup mascarpone cheese

1/2 teaspoon rose water

1/2 teaspoon vanilla extract

1/4 cup white sugar

Directions:

In a bowl, combine together the mascarpone cheese, sugar, rose water and vanilla.

Divide the strawberries into 4 dessert bowls. Add two dollops of mascarpone mixture on top and serve.

Chocolate Madeleines

Serves 12

Ingredients:

1/4 cup sifted flour

2 oz butter

1 egg

2 egg yolks

1/3 cup sugar

1/3 cup cocoa powder

1/2 tsp baking powder

a pinch of salt

1/2 tsp vanilla extract

1/2 cup powdered sugar, for dusting

Directions:

Sift the flour with cocoa, baking powder and salt in a large mixing bowl. In another bowl, beat the butter with the vanilla extract and the sugar. Mix in the egg and the egg yolks. Add in the dry ingredients, stirring, until just combined. Pour batter into buttered Madeleine shell forms.

Bake in a preheated to 375 F oven, for about 10 minutes. Remove from oven and immediately invert onto a wire rack to cool. Sprinkle with powdered sugar and serve.

French Fruit Cake

Serves 12

Ingredients:

1/2 cup butter, softened

1/2 cup sugar

2 1/2 tbsp honey

2 eggs

3/4 cup candied orange peel

1/2 cup candied lemon peel

1/2 cup raisins

1/2 cup walnuts, chopped

1 1/2 cups flour

1/2 tsp baking powder

1 1/2 tbsp milk

2 tbsp dark rum

1 tsp vanilla extract

Directions:

In a large bowl, beat the butter with the sugar and honey. Add in the eggs, the milk, rum, and vanilla extract. Stir in the remaining flour and the baking powder. Add the fruits and nuts and combine well. Turn the batter into a greased and floured 9 x 5 inch loaf pan.

Bake in a preheated to 350 F oven for 10 minutes. Lower the heat to 325 F and bake the cake for 40 minutes more, or until a toothpick comes out clean.

Easy Pear Tart

Serves 12

Ingredients:

1 cup butter, softened

1 cup sugar

4 eggs

2 cups flour

1 tsp baking powder

4 ripe pears, peeled and cubed

1 tsp vanilla extract

a pinch of salt

1 tsp lemon zest

Directions:

Grease a 9½ inch springform pan. Cream butter and sugar until very fluffy. Mix in the eggs slowly, one egg at a time. Add vanilla extract and lemon zest and stir. Add flour, baking powder and salt, stirring gently. Do not over mix.

Pour half of the batter into the pan then arrange the pears on top. Pour the rest of the batter over the pears. Bake in a preheated to 350 F oven for about 45 min or until a toothpick comes out clean.

Moist Apricot Muffins

Serves 16

Ingredients:

2 1/2 cups flour

1 cup white sugar

2 eggs

1 cup yogurt

1/2 cup milk

1/2 cup sunflower oil

2/3 cup apricots, chopped

1 tsp baking soda

1 tsp vanilla extract

1 tsp lemon zest

Preheat oven to 400 F. Grease 16 muffin cups or line with paper muffin liners.

Combine flour, sugar, chopped apricots, vanilla and baking soda in a large bowl. Whisk eggs, yogurt, milk, lemon zest and sunflower oil in another bowl until smooth; pour into dry mixture and stir until batter is just blended.

Fill prepared muffin cups 3/4 full and bake for 20 minutes or until a toothpick comes out clean. Cool in the pans for 10 minutes before removing to cool completely on a wire rack.

**FREE BONUS RECIPES: 10 Ridiculously Easy Jam and
Jelly Recipes Anyone Can Make**

A Different Strawberry Jam

Makes 6-7 11 oz jars

Ingredients:

4 lb fresh small strawberries (stemmed and cleaned)

5 cups sugar

1 cup water

2 tbsp lemon juice or 1 tsp citric acid

Directions:

Mix water and sugar and bring to the boil. Simmer sugar syrup for 5-6 minutes then slowly drop in the cleaned strawberries. Stir and bring to the boil again. Lower heat and simmer, stirring and skimming any foam off the top once or twice. Drop a small amount of the jam on a plate and wait a minute to see if it has thickened. If it has gelled enough, turn off the heat. If not, keep boiling and test every 5 minutes until ready. Two or three minutes before you remove the jam from the heat, add lemon juice or citric acid and stir well.

Ladle the hot jam in the jars until 1/8-inch from the top. Place the lid on top and flip the jar upside down. Continue until all of the jars are filled and upside down. Allow the jam to cool completely before turning right-side up. Press on the lid to check and see if it has sealed. If one of the jars lids doesn't pop up- the jar is not sealed–store it in a refrigerator.

Raspberry Jam

Makes 4-5 11 oz jars

Ingredients:

4 cups raspberries

4 cups sugar

1 tsp vanilla extract

1/2 tsp citric acid

Directions:

Gently wash and drain the raspberries. Lightly crush them with a potato masher, food mill or a food processor. Do not puree, it is better to have bits of fruit. Sieve half of the raspberry pulp to remove some of the seeds. Combine sugar and raspberries in a wide, thick-bottomed pot and bring mixture to a full rolling boil, stirring constantly. Skim any scum or foam that rises to the surface. Boil until the jam sets.

Test by putting a small drop on a cold plate – if the jam is set, it will wrinkle when given a small poke with your finger. Add citric acid, vanilla, and stir. Simmer for 2-3 minutes more, then ladle into hot jars. Flip upside down or process 10 minutes in boiling water.

Raspberry-Peach Jam

Makes 4-5 11 oz jars

Ingredients:

2 lb peaches

1 1/2 cup raspberries

4 cups sugar

1 tsp citric acid

Directions:

Wash and slice the peaches. Clean the raspberries and combine them with the peaches is a wide, heavy-bottomed saucepan. Cover with sugar and set aside for a few hours or overnight. Bring the fruit and sugar to a boil over medium heat, stirring occasionally. Remove any foam that rises to the surface.

Boil until the jam sets. Add citric acid and stir. Simmer for 2-3 minutes more, then ladle into hot jars. Flip upside down or process 10 minutes in boiling water.

Blueberry Jam

Makes 4-5 11 oz jars

Ingredients:

4 cups granulated sugar

3 cups blueberries (frozen and thawed or fresh)

3/4 cup honey

2 tbsp lemon juice

1 tsp lemon zest

Directions:

Gently wash and drain the blueberries. Lightly crush them with a potato masher, food mill or a food processor. Add the honey, lemon juice, and lemon zest, then bring to a boil over medium-high heat. Boils for 10-15 minutes, stirring from time to time. Boil until the jam sets.

Test by putting a small drop on a cold plate – if the jam is set, it will wrinkle when given a small poke with your finger. Skim off any foam, then ladle the jam into jars. Seal, flip upside down or process for 10 minutes in boiling water.

Triple Berry Jam

Makes 4-5 11 oz jars

Ingredients:

1 cup strawberries

1 cup raspberries

2 cups blueberries

4 cups sugar

1 tsp citric acid

Directions:

Mix berries and add sugar. Set aside for a few hours or overnight. Bring the fruit and sugar to the boil over medium heat, stirring frequently. Remove any foam that rises to the surface. Boil until the jam sets. Add citric acid, salt and stir.

Simmer for 2-3 minutes more, then ladle into hot jars. Flip upside down or process 10 minutes in boiling water.

Red Currant Jelly

Makes 6-7 11 oz jars

Ingredients:

2 lb fresh red currants

1/2 cup water

3 cups sugar

1 tsp citric acid

Directions:

Place the currants into a large pot, and crush with a potato masher or berry crusher. Add in water, and bring to a boil. Simmer for 10 minutes. Strain the fruit through a jelly or cheese cloth and measure out 4 cups of the juice. Pour the juice into a large saucepan, and stir in the sugar. Bring to full rolling boil, then simmer for 20-30 minutes, removing any foam that may rise to the surface. When the jelly sets, ladle in hot jars, flip upside down or process in boiling water for 10 minutes.

White Cherry Jam

Makes 3-4 11 oz jars

Ingredients:

2 lb cherries

3 cups sugar

2 cups water

1 tsp citric acid

Directions:

Wash and stone cherries. Combine water and sugar and bring to the boil. Boil for 5-6 minutes then remove from heat and add cherries. Bring to a rolling boil and cook until set. Add citric acid, stir and boil 1-2 minutes more.

Ladle in hot jars, flip upside down or process in boiling water for 10 minutes.

Cherry Jam

Makes 3-4 11 oz jars

Ingredients:

2 lb fresh cherries, pitted, halved

4 cups sugar

1/2 cup lemon juice

Directions:

Place the cherries in a large saucepan. Add sugar and set aside for an hour. Add the lemon juice and place over low heat. Cook, stirring occasionally, for 10 minutes or until sugar dissolves. Increase heat to high and bring to a rolling boil.

Cook for 5-6 minutes or until jam is set. Remove from heat and ladle hot jam into jars, seal and flip upside down.

Oven Baked Ripe Figs Jam

Makes 3-4 11 oz jars

Ingredients:

2 lb ripe figs

2 cups sugar

1 ½ cups water

2 tbsp lemon juice

Directions:

Arrange the figs in a Dutch oven, if they are very big, cut them in halves. Add sugar and water and stir well. Bake at 350 F for about one and a half hours. Do not stir. You can check the readiness by dropping a drop of the syrup in a cup of cold water – if it falls to the bottom without dissolving, the jam is ready. If the drop dissolves before falling, you can bake it a little longer. Take out of the oven, add lemon juice and ladle in the warm jars. Place the lids on top and flip the jars upside down. Allow the jam to cool completely before turning right-side up.

If you want to process the jams - place them into a large pot, cover the jars with water by at least 2 inches and bring to a boil. Boil for 10 minutes, remove the jars and sit to cool.

Quince Jam

Makes 5-6 11 oz jars

Ingredients:

4 lb quinces

5 cups sugar

2 cups water

1 tsp lemon zest

3 tbsp lemon juice

Directions:

Combine water and sugar in a deep, thick-bottomed saucepan and bring it to the boil. Simmer, stirring until the sugar has completely dissolved. Rinse the quinces, cut in half, and discard the cores.

Grate the quinces, using a cheese grater or a blender to make it faster. Quince flesh tends to darken very quickly, so it is good to do this as fast as possible. Add the grated quinces to the sugar syrup and cook uncovered, stirring occasionally until the jam turns pink and thickens to desired consistency, about 40 minutes.

Drop a small amount of the jam on a plate and wait a minute to see if it has thickened. If it has gelled enough, turn off the heat. If not, keep boiling and test every 2-3 minutes until ready. Two or three minutes before you remove the jam from the heat, add lemon juice and lemon zest and stir well.

Ladle in hot, sterilized jars and flip upside down.

About the Author

Vesela lives in Bulgaria with her family of six (including the Jack Russell Terrier). Her passion is going green in everyday life and she loves to prepare homemade cosmetic and beauty products for all her family and friends.

Vesela has been publishing her cookbooks for over a year now. If you want to see other healthy family recipes that she has published, together with some natural beauty books, you can check out her Author Page on Amazon.

33008686R00081

Printed in Great Britain
by Amazon